DISCOVERING ECUADOR

and the Galapagos Islands

PRECEDING PAGE
Clothing and ornaments of a Cañari Indian
girl symbolize her people's persistence in
keeping alive their indigenous ways.

THIS PAGE
In the northern Andean highlands, the cold
wind of the dry season rakes Olmedo's
little burial ground. In June, when the hills
turn yellow, songs of harvest echo from
distant mountainsides. Rural fiestas recall
the cycle of life.

DISCOVERING ECUADOR
and the Galapagos Islands

Imprenta Mariscal ✍ Dinediciones

University of Missouri
School of Journalism

This project was made possible through the generous assistance of

The President of Ecuador
Metropolitan Touring
Saeta Airlines
Kodak-Comandato S.A.

Copyright ©1994
PABLO CORRAL
and LOUP LANGTON;
Photographs copyright
©1994 photographers et al.;
prologue copyright
©1994 Loren McIntyre

Editorial Directors:
PABLO CORRAL
LOUP LANGTON

Producer:
CARMEN HERRERA

Assistant Producer:
LYNN E. MILLER

Accounting:
ALBERTO BORBÓN
WENCESLÁO PUENTE

Project Assistants:
MARÍA CISNEROS
CRISTÓBAL CORRAL
FLORENCIA MENA
ROHANNA MERTENS
JULIA ORTEGA

Picture Editors:
JAN COLBERT
University of Missouri

MIKE DAVIS
National Geographic Society

KENT KOBERSTEEN
National Geographic Society

LELLO PIAZZA
Airone Magazine, Italy

SYLVIE REBBOT
GEO Magazine, France

KATHY RYAN
*New York Times Sunday
Magazine*

FRANCISCO VALDIVIESO
Imprenta Mariscal

Captions Editors:
PABLO CORRAL
LOREN McINTYRE
BYRON SCOTT
University of Missouri

Design Editor:
KATE GLASSNER
BRAINERD

Production Assistant:
ELIZABETH A. DOHERTY

Prologue Writer:
LOREN McINTYRE

Published by
IMPRENTA MARISCAL,
DINEDICIONES and
UNIVERISTY OF
MISSOURI
SCHOOL OF JOURNALISM

First printing
October 1994

PRINTED IN ECUADOR
Grupo Imprenta Mariscal
Fax (5932) 449 713
Quito, Ecuador

General Manager
& Publisher
FRANCISCO VALDIVIESO

Pre-press
PATRICIO CRIOLLO

Color Separations
JOSE TORRES

Stripping
WALTER TORRES

Press
HERNÁN CRIOLLO

Binding
MARCO PAZMIÑO

Library of Congress
Cataloging-in-publication Data:
Descubriendo Ecuador
Produced by Pablo Corral
and Loup Langton;
the photographers et al.;
the writer Loren McIntyre.

ISBN 0-9644049-0-7

38 photographers from eleven countries

in four continents were dispatched throughout Ecuador to contribute their work to *Discovering Ecuador and the Galapagos Islands*. Each photographer was assigned to a particular area of the country, and the group produced approximately 66,000 photographs in one week. A team of picture editors from around the world met in Quito and edited the photographs. After a painstaking week of editing, 162 images were chosen for this book. The photographers:

François Ancellet	Melissa Farlow	Daniele Pellegrini
Jorge Juan Anhalzer	Denis Finley	Peter Pfersick
Mariana Bazo	Bolo Franco	Eduardo Quintana
Alan Berner	César Franco	Susie Post
Yann Arthus-Bertrand	Marcela García	Raghu Rai
Jim Blair	Santiago Harker	David Rees
Alberto Borbón	Jeremy Horner	Guido Alberto Rossi
Aldo Brando	Michio Hoshino	Diego Samper
Judy Bustamante	Loup Langton	Paula Simas
Fabián Cevallos	Pascal Maitre	Scott Thode
Diego Cifuentes	Michele McDonald	Matteo Torri
Pablo Corral	Robert Mertens	Carmen Troesser
Peter Essick	Randy Olson	

La Sierra

The Mountains

Highland fields of grain, in Hacienda Zuleta, lie almost two miles above sea level in the northern province of Imbabura. The Andes warp the tropical terrain of Ecuador, lifting the middle of the country into frigid air aloft, and thus creating climatic zones that range from equatorial to polar.

Four generations of women
occupy the same home in a
colonial district of Quito:
(from left to right) Anita
Granja (hands), Mercedes
de Granja, Victoria Salazar
and little Karina. The
extended family, with mem-
bers from both mother's
and father's sides, forms
the core of a society rooted
in Roman Catholicism.

Every day, before and after school, Raul Vimos shines shoes in the plaza outside San Francisco church in the center of colonial Quito. The construction of San Francisco began in 1534 on the site of the garrison of Huayna Capac, the third and last Inca emperor. The artistic treasures of this church and others led UNESCO to name the historic center of Quito a World Heritage Site.

The Rain Forest

The Oriente of Ecuador,
part of the 2,700,000-square-
mile basin of the Amazon
River, is saturated with
some of the heaviest rainfall
on earth. Prevailing east-
west winds from the Atlantic
Ocean draw moisture from
the rain forest while cross-
ing the continent. The
winds drive clouds against
the eastern slope of the
Andes; the clouds rise into
cooler atmosphere and con-
dense into rain. Waters
from both rain and melted
snow cascade down the
slopes until they reach the
relative quiet of flatland
rivers and lagoons such as
this: Imuya Lake in
Cuyabeno Wildlife Reserve.

The life of Delfín Payaguaje, a Secoya Indian of the Aguarico River region in the Oriente's Sucumbíos Province, differs little from that of his rain-forest ancestors. For riverine peoples speaking various native languages, the forest is the homeland for their pre-Columbian culture.

LAS GALÁPAGOS

Galapagos Islands

A torpid column of marine iguanas heads for the sea across the sands of Punta Espinosa, on Fernandina Island, in Galapagos National Park. Few of the strange and fascinating wild creatures of the archipelago fear humankind. Charles Darwin's observation of their unique differences from island to island led to a major innovation of natural science. His 1837 journal says, "greatly struck (by) character of South American fossils and species on Galapagos Archipelago. These facts, especially latter, (are the) origin of all my views."

Holding to time-tested techniques, fishermen dry and repair their shrimp nets in Olmedo, Esmeraldas Province, on Ecuador's northern coast. Nilber Valverde, Guardo Gambindo, Manuel Ortiz and Adela Perea (from left to right) learned the art from their fathers. The nation's major income from shrimp is derived from a large deep-sea fishing fleet and the cultivation of shrimp in enormous artificial ponds.

After an unusual wedding ceremony combining a nuptial Mass and their daughter's baptism, Luis, Berta, and their ring-bearers leave the little church of Puerto Hualtaco in El Oro Province.

Contents

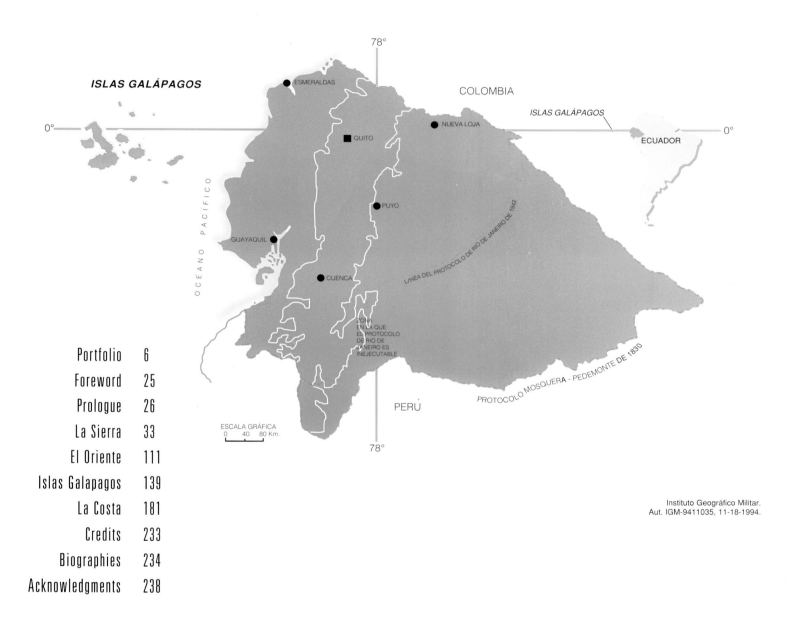

ISLAS GALÁPAGOS

COLOMBIA

ESMERALDAS

ISLAS GALÁPAGOS

ECUADOR

NUEVA LOJA

QUITO

PUYO

OCÉANO PACÍFICO

GUAYAQUIL

CUENCA

LÍNEA DEL PROTOCOLO DE RÍO DE JANEIRO DE 1942

ZONA EN LA QUE EL PROTOCOLO DE RÍO DE JANEIRO ES INEJECUTABLE

PROTOCOLO MOSQUERA - PEDEMONTE DE 1830

PERÚ

ESCALA GRÁFICA
0   40   80 Km.

78°

78°

0°

0°

Instituto Geográfico Militar.
Aut. IGM-9411035, 11-18-1994.

Foreword

BY LOUP LANGTON

This book is about an extraordinary country on the Pacific coast of South America, and it's about an international group of photographers and editors' love for their craft. But, more than anything "Discovering Ecuador and the Galapagos Islands" is about working together across cultures with all of its inherent frustrations, joys, anger—passion.

The project began in Pablo Corral's Quito apartment in August, 1993. I was preparing to return to the United States after spending three months of teaching, photographing and exploring in Ecuador. Pablo and I began talking about the possibility of working on a modest project together for the following summer. Six hours of discussion later we had put together a proposal that included bringing photographers and editors from around the world for the purpose of creating a book about Ecuador. The next morning we went to visit the person who could make that plan a reality, Paco Valdivieso. Paco is the general manager of Imprenta Mariscal, our publisher and printer; he is also a visionary. We told him that we needed financial support, but we wanted to retain editorial control. We also told him that there would be no profits since we were interested in using the income to establish a fund to assist Ecuadorian photographers in their work. Paco's only reply was, "we'll do it together."

And, we did do it together. It was a strange and wonderful gathering of people for a common purpose. Ecuadorian sponsors from the President's office to tour agencies, airlines and cruise lines had their own expectations and hopes for the contents of the book. Most North American and several European photographers and editors, coming from journalism backgrounds, had very different ideas about the kind of book it should be. And, a few Ecuadorian photographers wondered why there were so many gringos participating.

These disparate viewpoints were reflected in the discussions between the directors of the project. Pablo, Paco and I quarreled intermittently throughout the summer, only to reach consensus and then quarrel again. These disagreements were out of passion—passion for Ecuador, passion for photography, passion for one's own cultural perspective.

Perhaps the most important discovery of all for those of us who participated in the Ecuador project is the realization that we can love and appreciate others for their cultural differences and for their zeal in preserving those differences.

Prologue

BY LOREN McINTYRE

A latent volcano, Cayambe, 18,996 feet elevation, stands on the Equator.

Years ago I traveled in Ecuador for four months on assignment for the *National Geographic* magazine, taking thousands of pictures and seeing all I could see from peasants to president, from diving underwater with sea lions to climbing snow peaks under starlight. I enjoyed those months so much that every journey to Ecuador afterwards holds for me the aura of pilgrimage. I thought that turning the pages of this book would treat me to little more than remembrances of this promised land. But I was wrong; much of this book is a revelation to me—especially the candid glimpses into private lives.

In their spontaneity, many of the illustrations are the antitheses of an overarching view I took of the country from an Ecuadorian Air Force jet bomber. Often, when Quito was sunny, I went to the airport hoping to fly and capture on film a panorama of Ecuador's snow peaks—all but one of them volcanoes—with a single exposure. I reasoned that the Sierra, the mountainous region, was the very spine of Ecuador in more ways than geographical; that the nation's cultural past and present were inextricably linked to the central highlands in ways akin to the nervous system of vertebrates. But time and again clouds from the Amazon side of the highlands wreathed most of the peaks. As my pilot said, "The mountains are very coquettish. Seldom do they all unveil themselves at once."

On the seventeenth try I got lucky; 6 September 1966 dawned cloudless throughout Ecuador. I lay prone in the Plexiglas nose of a Canberra, my heartbeat accelerating at take-off since my eyes were barely a meter above the runway. Upon reaching 40,000 feet altitude I heard on the intercom an almost ancestral chant as the copilot recited the array of mountains seen from north to south, "Cayambe, Sara Urco, Antisana, Cotopaxi, Chimborazo, Tungurahua, El Altar, Sangay." Through a clear panel of optical glass I could see the mountains he named, as well as plantations reaching west to the Pacific Ocean, and, to the east, a chlorophyll carpet of treetops unrolling to flat infinity. But of course I could not see any people, such as those whose faces appeal to you from these pages, when I flew above the mountains named for gods.

The peaks resemble volcanoes of the Pacific Northwest's Cascade Range, but Ecuador's volcanoes average a mile higher than the Cascades. Chimborazo's summit snows were once thought to be the loftiest on earth, and in a sense they are. Due to its position on the spinning globe's equatorial bulge, Chimborazo's 20,703-foot-high crest, measured from the center of the globe instead of sea level, is two miles higher than Mount Everest.

About half of Ecuador's eleven million people live among the volcanoes. I scaled Cotopaxi in the days when rural folk believed it was hunting for buried Inca treasure that drove occasional strangers to risk death seeking it on mountain tops. It seemed to me quite a feat at that time—especially since I did it without proper equipment—to join the then-small company of climbers who had attained Cotopaxi's exhaustingly high summit. At 19,347 feet altitude a breath of air holds less than half as much oxygen as at sea level. Nowadays, groups of urban schoolmates sometimes succeed in reaching the summit crater on weekend excursions. Yet it is arduous, dangerous, and quite impossible after a snowfall when fluffy chest-deep drifts, hidden crevasses, and risk of avalanche deter even the experts.

Somewhere on the south slope of Cayambe I once stepped from summer into winter—and that is not a play on words, since the equatorial line crosses a glacier there. It is the only place on the earth's surface where both latitude and temperature reach zero.

The most spectacular of the six active Ecuadorian volcanoes is Sangay, the southernmost, which has never been known to cease erupting. Climbers woo and may win sudden death on its ashen slopes, a no-man's-land frequently bombarded by twisted blobs of molten magma that explode from its crater, sizzle in random trajectories, and plunge into its steep snow fields. Sangay's Fujiesque cone is seldom visible, even to its reckless climbers, because of heavy clouds laid upon it by Amazonian winds.

All of the great mountains were holy places worshipped by the Incas who ruled Ecuador before the Spanish conquistadors came. The Incas called their emperor Intipchuri, Son of the Sun. They worshipped the Sun as the leading deity under Viracocha, the Creator, author of all life—a creed not very distant from that of people today who believe in a Supreme Being while also recognizing that the sun is the genesis of all life on earth.

This book bears witness to the pervading power of sunlight—particularly that which fell on Ecuador during a few days in the middle of 1994—as you shall see in the pages that follow. It also illustrates the virtuosity of the human eye, an organ so sensitive that it can respond, unaided, to a stimulus of 1/100 trillionth of a watt, as when focused on a star thousands of light-years distant. The eye can accommodate objects a million times brighter—although it cannot look directly without damage at a relatively small star, a very near one, only eight light-minutes away: the sun. It is reflected sunlight that lets the eye perceive its outdoor surroundings.

Around 400 BC. Democritus—a founder of the atomic theory—thought that the ability to see came of illuminated objects giving off faint copies of themselves, delivered to the mind. Democritus would appreciate this book, for these pages hold not-so-faint copies of the visual experience of photographers whose 38 pairs of eyes looked upon the land and peered into the many faces of Ecuador. Their images reach your mind through photographic and printing processes the Greek philosopher could not have imagined although he summarized them nicely, 2400 years ago.

For an example of how these processes work, consider photographer Peter Essick. We find him traveling the beaches of Esmeraldas Province, a region where aging adventurer Francisco Pizarro landed with 180 men and 27 horses in 1531, determined to find the Inca Empire and make it his own. The sun is shining on some fishermen—or, put more scientifically, a broad spectrum of electromagnetic energy radiating from the sun is falling

Somewhere on the south slope of Cayambe I once stepped from summer into winter—and that is not a play on words, since the equatorial line crosses a glacier there. It is the only place on the earth's surface where both latitude and temperature reach zero.

upon the planet: some frequencies are absorbed, but most of the energy in the visual spectrum, that octave of frequencies from violet to red perceptible to the human eye, is reflected from water, clouds, and, in this instance, the fishermen and their catch. Peter eyes the fishermen. Since he is seeking examples of north coast people to illustrate this book and sunlight reflected from a catch of sardine-size fish has caught his attention, he moves in. He lifts a camera, looks through a finder, and presses a button to allow the light to strike a film sensitized to the same range of frequencies that his eyes perceive. Then, having made on the spot his own editorial decision that this subject is better for the book than others he has seen, he moves in closer and repeats the shot from many angles with several lenses.

Of the 66,000 pictures submitted by all 38 photographers, one color slide of Peter's fishermen survived a winnowing process in which seven picture editors from four nations chose nearly 200 images fit for a book dedicated to the pictorial discovery of modern Ecuador. Then designer Kate Glassner Brainerd, working in North America, decided upon the sizes, sequences and design of images. Peter's fishermen slide, as well as the others, was sent to the print shop in Quito where it was separated photographically into three basic colors, transferred to larger sheets of film, and then to metal. Finally, it was inked in color onto paper coated with kaolin, a white clay, for maximum reflectivity.

If you open this book in daylight to pages 182-183, you may see the fishermen with their catch as Peter Essick saw them when he prowled Esmeraldas. The light of day around you, wherever you are, is reflected from the colored ink into your eye in one nano-second. Some light filters through the ink and bounces back from the shiny surface of the paper underneath, gathering more color. The image leaps from the page at a speed of 186,282 miles per second, enters your brain through the miracle of sight, and perhaps becomes knowledge.

I can only guess at the doubts and decisions of the photographers assigned to various regions of Ecuador as they

Morning mist rises from Caño Iripari, in Cuyabeno National Park.

worked at gathering pictures for this book, but perhaps they resembled my own qualms, as told in the prologue to my book "Exploring South America:"

"While shooting country stories I am never sure what to look for. On the road I sometimes feel dislocated in time and space from the opportunity for a big picture. I speed past a thatched hut at the edge of a forest, beguiled by a glimpse of a girl poised at her window, hands crossed on the sill. The scene fades behind me and the second thoughts begin. Had I indeed seen a Gioconda smile and eyes like emeralds set in cinnamon? If I had caught it on film, might her portrait hang one day in the wardroom of some future spaceship? Why hurry on, why not stop? Regret grows stronger and finally wrenches me around. I hurry back several miles. But, as in a nightmare, darkness falls before I get there; she is nowhere to be seen.

"The perfect picture—if there is such a thing—forever eludes me for shortage of time, for lack of luck, or for poverty of artistic vision. Or maybe for failure to seek divine grace, as was required of the knights errant of Arthurian legend. Wandering the wilderness in search of the ultimate photograph can be as unfulfilling as their quest for the Holy Grail."

My own quest? It is for images that might excite a sense of wonder. I seek to record things that few people would otherwise get to see (birds that nest behind a hidden waterfall) or that are about to disappear forever (an Indian boy in the rain forest carrying his tribal ancestor, a beautiful parrot, on his shoulder). If the opportunity disappears or the picture doesn't come out, I grieve inordinately.

The feeling of loss vanishes whenever I listen to someone who typifies the culture I'm trying to record, such as Julian

Muinala. Julian is headman of Peguche, a hamlet in the northern highlands near a waterfall whose sunlit spray creates rainbows alleged to violate virgins. Like his people's menfolk, Don Julian wears Otavalan clothing: rope-soled slippers, spic-and-span white culottes, blue or gray poncho, felt hat, and a long braided pigtail. He is an elder of the Muinala Lema family, master weavers, who claim descendence from tribal chieftains who resisted the Incas, and then the Spaniards. They cultivated tilted farmland high on Imbabura, a sacred volcano, green almost to its black stone crest. Even in distant times almost every Otavalan cottage had a Spanish wooden loom on its verandah. The men wove and the women—elegantly dressed in long dark skirts and embroidered white blouses with multiple strands of gilt beads— were the financial managers. Soon Otavalan men and women in native dress were peddling piles of ponchos and shawls on street corners from New York to Buenos Aires and even selling woolens to denizens of the sweltering Amazon. One of Julian's sons lived in Barcelona, Spain, and two others in Los Angeles, California.

Julian said, "My family operates looms all over Colombia. Also in Caracas, the Canary Islands, and Bahia, Brazil. If everyone comes home at once, they'll have to sleep in the streets. With the profits we used to buy farmland. Now there's none available around here. So we're into retail stores. My son Alonso and his wife María Elena own a record shop and a restaurant up north in Ibarra."

In the northern Ecuadorian highlands one may see smartly dressed Otavalans riding taxis driven by whites along the Pan-American Highway. This main thoroughfare, called the Pana, threads the mountains from Colombia to Peru. It was made of cobblestones when I first knew it. The cobbles followed—and erased—remains of the ancient Inca road through Ecuador.

The fields of Topo in Imbabura Province after the barley and corn harvest.

Today, it's straighter and swifter of surface.

In 1547, only fifteen years after Pizarro captured and executed the Ecuador-born Inca Atahuallpa, bringing about the fall of the Empire, an alert and literate Spaniard rode down the Inca highway with paper, ink, and quill pen in his saddlebags. Pedro de Cieza de Leon was not only the most reliable of the chroniclers but also one of the first discoverers of Ecuador since (according to Webster) "to discover" is "to make known." Cieza described for his king and commoners the fascinating peoples he met and recorded the names of the principal native communities he passed on his way to fight in the Spanish civil war in Peru. Amazingly, many of them are now towns and cities where photographers who worked on the highlands portion of this book were based: Yaguarcocha (Blood Lake), Otavalo, Guallabamba, Quito, Latacunga, Ambato, Riobamba, Cañar, Tomebamba (Cuenca), and Loja.

Many intersections along the Pana are cultural crossroads still today, with differences in dress and native tongues that Cieza described some 20 generations ago. Some of the populations were mitimaes, reliable settlers brought by the Incas from other parts of the Empire as far away as the Bolivian shores of Lake Titicaca, in exchange for troublesome local tribes that resented Inca rule. The mitimaes brought with them peanuts, potatoes, llamas, and the Quichua language. The remaining local tribes were brainwashed; taught to comply with Inca ways and forsake their own languages for Quichua. Even now, traces of that long-ago transculturization appear in the hinterlands, such as distinctive headgear that reveals indigenous origins.

In the volcanic central provinces of Tungurahua and Chimborazo, ash and pumice streak the higher hillsides in patterned shades like Scottish woolens from the Hebrides, while the lower slopes are color checkerboards of crops, yellow, green, and tan. Night comes swiftly in this equatorial countryside. But south of Cuenca, where the ranges open to the west, sunsets may last a while if high cloud cover reaches from the mountains to someplace far at sea. As the sun dips into the Pacific beyond the edge of the cloud, orange light enters the clear layer of air between sea and sky and reflects back into the sierra for perhaps an hour.

This region was invaded by Tupa Inca, the second emperor, after he succeeded his father, Pachacuti (cataclysm) around 1471. Marching more than 1,200 miles north of Cuzco, where the urge to empire had been conceived and nurtured, he named Quito his northern capital. Five years after Tupa Inca's reign ended, with his mummy enshrined in the catacomb of his forebearers in Cuzco, a Spaniard named Sebastian de Benalcázar sailed westward on Columbus' third voyage. In 1534, during the wars of conquest, Benalcazar founded the Villa de San Francisco de Quito on the rubble of the earlier capital.

Having escaped the devastation and looting of modern warfare, Quito is a colonial treasure house; its churches, most ornate of any in the hemisphere, will attract worshippers well into the 21st century, as photographer Susie Post suggests on pages 72-73. I stand amazed that the city retains so well its colonial charm since it has doubled in population to 1.2 million in the 28 years since *National Geographic* published my Ecuador article. However, to the north, scores of high-rise condominiums now line the narrow crest of the ridge above Guápulo and climb the slopes of Volcan Pichincha, while to the south the citizenry lives rather less loftily.

Spaniards from Quito, fellow conquistadors of the city's founder, led a horde of Indians, hogs, llamas, and dogs down the eastern watershed of the Andes in 1541 to search for

Imagine looking from space at earth's Western Hemisphere with the sun over your right shoulder and the west coast of South America still in shadow. At the edge of darkness, Ecuador, a triangular speck of land equidistant from both North and South Poles, circles eastward toward daylight with the rotation of the earth.

El Dorado and the Land of Cinnamon. It took an unhappy year of hacking through one of the thickest and wettest forests on earth for them to reach Amazon headwaters deep enough to float a boat. Some of the famished Spaniards became the first to descend the Amazon to the sea, laying the foundation for the claim, now set in stone, that "Ecuador has been, is, and always will be an Amazonian country." I realized how miserable it must have been for those obsessed Spaniards to invade Ecuador's Oriente when I met in 1947 some naval officers, both Ecuadorian and Peruvian, who were surveying the boundary between their two countries. Several suffered from tropical diseases; one had the bridge of his nose eaten away by leishmaniasis.

Had the conquistadors been able to view from on high the Oriente's unbroken expanse of rain forest, they would have seen only watery glints warning of alien things, perilous to horse and steel-jacketed rider. Five centuries would pass before explorers learned that the riches of Ecuador's Oriente were hidden not in a glistening palace but in the subsoil. Oil prospectors had been hunting the treasure for years. I took many pictures of their search but the black liquid didn't come gushing out of the ground until a year after I left. The appearance of the dark riches when released is less than lustrous, as photographer Diego Samper shows on page 129. Yet petroleum products affect the lives of everyone and to use them is to recover some of the energy of sunlight that fell on earth when it was young.

Imagine looking from space at earth's Western Hemisphere with the sun over your right shoulder and the west coast of South America still in shadow. At the edge of darkness, Ecuador, a triangular speck of land equidistant from both North and South Poles, circles eastward toward daylight with the rotation of the earth. Riding the bulge of the oblate spheroid,

Ecuador travels farther every day—and faster, a thousand miles an hour—than anyplace closer to the poles. Energy streaming from the sun sweeps across the cloud-wreathed continent. It soon brings morning to the rain forest of the Oriente as Ecuador comes out of the dark.

With the arrival of daylight, the chlorophyll that greens the rain forest canopy begins to absorb the solar energy essential to life on earth, using water and carbon dioxide to create carbohydrates and free oxygen. This photosynthesis is the only counterbalance on the continents to burning, decomposition, and death. It is the catalyst that creates the trees. If not burned down, the Oriente's forests could themselves become petroleum in a future geologic age, after time and an infinity of microbes have accomplished their alchemy.

For now, for me, it is enough to revel in the riches of the rain forest, to wonder about the yet unknown forms of life in the canopy, and to trust that they will not be sacrificed to ephemeral needs.

As the wheeling earth draws continental Ecuador into morning, darkness still conceals its outlying Archipelago de Colon, now termed the Galapagos Islands. Half an hour later, daybreak comes to that fabulous sanctuary. Some of its landscapes appear to be extra-terrestrial; its wildlife bizarre. Michio Hoshino shows you some monsters, imps of darkness as Darwin called them, on pages 146-147. Had Christopher Columbus, great discoverer of islands, made landfall in 1492 on this archipelago named for him, his sailors would have had confirmed their worst fears of dragons at the world's end.

Galapagos has also harbored peculiar humans. Margaret Wittmer, long a resident of Floreana Island, once told me of the shocking death by poison of her vegetarian neighbor with steel teeth, of a volcanic eruption which swallowed a bomber, and of a missing baroness and her courtiers dead of thirst. The tales weren't altogether news to me; I had read them in Sunday supplements of Seattle newspapers when I was in high school—such was the lurid fame of Galapagos in the 1930s. Another time I tried and failed to climb 5,600-foot-high Wolf Volcano, on the big island, Isabela, to photograph land iguanas. The equatorial line bisects Wolf's crater.

In the same decade that Charles Darwin's studies of Galapagos wildlife helped to explain evolution, the remote equatorial archipelago became Ecuadorian territory, claimed by General Jose Villamil and annexed by Guayas Province in 1832.

The annexation was a natural act by the outward-looking citizens of La Costa, the Pacific provinces of Ecuador west of the Andes. Many think of themselves as seafarers: a fisherman hauling in a net full of sea bass, a stevedore loading passion fruit containers consigned to Denmark, or a shipping executive consulting a marine chronometer mounted on his mahogany office wall. Almost all the forefathers of costeños—other than the purely indigenous ones—originally came to Ecuador from across the sea. Perhaps the thought processes of costeños tend to differ somewhat from those of Atahuallpas, as they term the highland people. The ocean, not the mountains, is in the costeños'

The odor of cane fields permeates Salinas valley, in Imbabura Province.

blood. I sympathize with that, for I, too, was born at the water's edge, and I've gone to sea so much of my life I've lost count of the voyages, even those that put into Guayaquil.

The historic rivalry between Guayaquil and Quito is quickly perceived by most observers—including those who helped build this book. Whether or not their differences breed success, their disparate styles are certainly less tedious than the concentration of wealth and power in a single great city, as in 14 other Latin American countries where I've worked. Here on the equator, power is polarized but not cloned. Quito's power is in the ministries; Guayaquil's is in the banks. For generations Quito has been more traditional, conservative, and insular, while Guayaquil is more contemporary, liberal, and worldly. An urbane outlook also seems characteristic of the southern seaport Machala, Ecuador's fourth largest city, the "banana capital of the world."

Since the founding of the republic, one product after another—some of them unusual—has been at or near the top of the export trade. The growth of all of them has depended upon the direct impact of rays from the fiery star the Incas adored: toquilla fiber for weaving Panama hats, tagua nuts for carving vegetable-ivory buttons, balsa wood for building models, kapok for filling lifejackets, cacao, rice, coffee, bananas, and now, the farming of shrimp and flowers.

As Ecuador is a truly civilized country, long free of war and pestilence, I believe its leading trade will soon be tourism—which is now fourth, after oil, bananas, and shrimp. You can usually count on the man or woman in the streets of Ecuador to return your "Buenos dias" with a smile no matter where you come from—a very rare virtue as this century ends.

Where I grew up, the argument of where to go on vacation, whether mountains or seashore, was so wrenching that it used to be the subject of comic strips. Today, a tourist in Ecuador doesn't have to belabor such a decision, considering the ease of enjoying Cotopaxi National Park one day and sunning on a Guayas beach the next—plus a third option, the opportunity to visit the upper edge of the world's greatest tropical forest. Where else on earth can one experience all the world's climates within a few minutes flight or a few hours drive? Or visit the other-worldly wildlife of Galapagos just a short flight away?

Ecuador, a nation the size of Nevada, is often termed "a small country," but that is a New World point of view. In Europe, twenty nations are smaller. Ecuador is truly large in the majesty of its landscapes and the heterogeneity of all forms of life therein. Ecuador is many countries in a little space.

Therefore, looking at this book is like reading Christopher Columbus' letters to his king describing his discovery of the Indies by sailing west. Columbus' story, while utterly fascinating, leaves untold the marvels of the American continents that lay beyond his ken. Although the many photographers who worked directly on this book were gifted with singular sight, they left untold the marvels of Ecuador that lay beyond their lenses. They could not pretend to capture even a millionth of the country on film, considering that small as it may seem, 110,000 square miles is too much territory to cover in a lifetime. The photographers were forced to choose, each in his or her own way, what to photograph; they had to "edit in the field."

And so it is that even though the picture-takers and the editors have been able to put between the covers of this book an invitation to the discovery of Ecuador, you can never learn what it is really like until you accept their invitation, travel the land, talk to the people, and discover the splendors and sorrows of Ecuador for yourself. ■

LA SIERRA

The Mountains

El Quinche rests after an exhausting day of receiving pilgrims. Thousands, of all social levels, gather in this village near Quito to pray to Our Lady of El Quinche.

Beside the isolated road from El Quinche to Cangahua, northeast of Quito, a sister, two brothers, and two dogs huddle against the cold highland winds. At these altitudes, hardy livestock and subsistence agriculture barely sustain life.

Although growth of the nation's capital threatens to devour the small towns roundabout, Uyumbicho maintains its character despite its nearness to Quito. Little general stores in these towns often stay open to serve nocturnal travelers.

Santo Domingo church, beyond the busy Avenida 24 de Mayo,
attracts the largest attendance of Quito's faithful.

In Quito, Galo Mora, a musician of the group "Pueblo Nuevo,"
tells a bedtime story to his son Martín.

In Quito, cadets of Eloy Alfaro military academy begin calisthenics at daybreak.

Rosario Tigre goes home to prepare dinner. Her community in
Azuay Province, near Cuenca, was destroyed by flood in 1993.

Lorenza de Jerez grooms her husband Pablo, in Salasaca,
Tungurahua Province. Legend holds that the Incas transferred
Salasacans to Ecuador from Bolivia in the fifteenth century.

"Why not take a picture of someone better looking?" asks a man watching dancers during the Fiesta de San Pedro in Cayambe.

At a sweater factory in Otavalo, Celio Guerrero spins wool while Segundo Oyagata weaves on the loom. Most of the textiles sold at the famous Otavalo market and sold around the world by Otavalan peddlers are products of cottage industries such as this.

Toa Andrango of Topochico, a village in Imbabura Province, prepares chicha for celebrants of the midyear festival of San Juan. Chicha, a corn beer, has been drunk in enormous quantities in the Andes since pre-Inca times.

Sheep dogs help herd a flock in Chimborazo Province. The sale of woolen textiles has earned income for highlanders ever since sheep were brought to the New World by the earliest Spanish colonists.

Resplendent in his "suit of lights," a torero maintains a classic stance as he leads the swift shadow of a fighting bull past his steadfast feet with a flick of his red muleta. The deadly ballet of the bullfight, introduced from Spain in colonial times, is still performed at indigenous festivals such as the San Pedro - San Pablo harvest ritual every June 29 in Cayambe.

A tethered rooster, symbol of fertility, is carried in procession through Hacienda Zuleta on the slopes of Volcan Imbabura, just above the equator. After an oration by a boy on horseback, the rooster will be offered by the campesinos to the landowner as a token of respect on the day of San Juan. A world-renowned president of Ecuador, Galo Plaza Lasso, who once owned the 6,000-acre hacienda, pioneered programs of health, education, and land grants to end the historic serfdom of its indigenous population.

Elaborate blouses of the
Castro sisters identify them
as natives of Imbabura
Province. Regional
differences in dress, food,
and dance have persisted
since colonial times.

Paintings by Eduardo Kingman often feature oversized hands of stylized figures. Since the 1930s, Kingman—now entering his ninth decade—has pioneered Ecuador's "indigenism" school, exploring native themes of tenderness and sorrow in murals, canvasses, and book illustrations.

Quito, capital of Ecuador, crowds a ledge on the eastern slope
of 15,728-foot Mount Pichincha. As the sun sets behind the
volcano, a brief dusk warms the northern reaches of the city
where new high-rises belie the city's essentially colonial nature.

Miguel Pandám, leader of
the Indigenous Federation
of the Shuar Peoples, is
escorted out of the
Government Palace after a
discussion that led to a new
agreement on land reform.
Political rivalries that used
to breed violence in Ecuador
now tend to be settled by
more peaceful means.

People of all ages get together at the Pobre Diablo (Poor Devil), one of Quito's many night spots.

Ecuador's National Symphony Orchestra performs weekly at the
Teatro Sucre and often features guest soloists from abroad.

Farmlands in Zumbabua, Cotopaxi Province, nearly reach the peaks. Most of the broad bowl-shaped valleys, cultivated for centuries, have retained their fertility in spite of shallow topsoil barely covering deep layers of volcanic ash. Most of the native Andean forests in this region were cut down for cooking and ritual fires long before Europeans arrived. Eucalyptus trees were imported from Australia a century ago.

A burro burdened by dried sugar cane used for cattle feed heads homeward along a mountain road in the southern province of Loja. Donkeys introduced by the Spaniards gradually replaced the Incas' beloved llamas because they carry heavier loads and even people.

Women weave hats of "toquilla" straw, derived from the leaves of jipijapa plants, "Carludovica palmata," in the southern town of Sigsig, Azuay Province. This cottage industry has survived intact from the seventeenth century.

Cañar, in high country that the Incas favored, is the farming center of Cañar Province. A chronicler wrote that to defeat the long-haired Cañari in the fifteenth century, the Inca army mustered 200,000 soldiers –possibly counting wives and camp followers. On a hillside not far from Cañar stands Ingapirca, the finest Inca structure in all Ecuador.

During the fiesta of San Pedro, patron saint of Cayambe, secluded households of Cayambe open their doors to Indian musicians and dancers. Cane liquor loosens their tongues, animates their fingers and limbers their legs.

San Francisco church remains a jewel of baroque architecture, richly ornamented with gold leaf, despite having suffered repeated earthquakes and rebuilding. Its doors remain open, and its opulent colonial treasures, that elsewhere might have been carried off to museums, continue to form part of the daily life of Quito's religious communities.

Cloistered Carmelite nuns at Carmen Bajo Monastery, out of sight of the congregation behind the curtain, hear morning Mass. Roman Catholicism, the faith of most Ecuadorians, suffers from modern society's secular trends. Few young people wish to devote their lives to hard monastic discipline.

The lifetimes of Carmelite nuns, highlighted only by rites of joint prayer, are totally secluded from the boisterousness of contemporary Quito that lies beyond the convent walls.

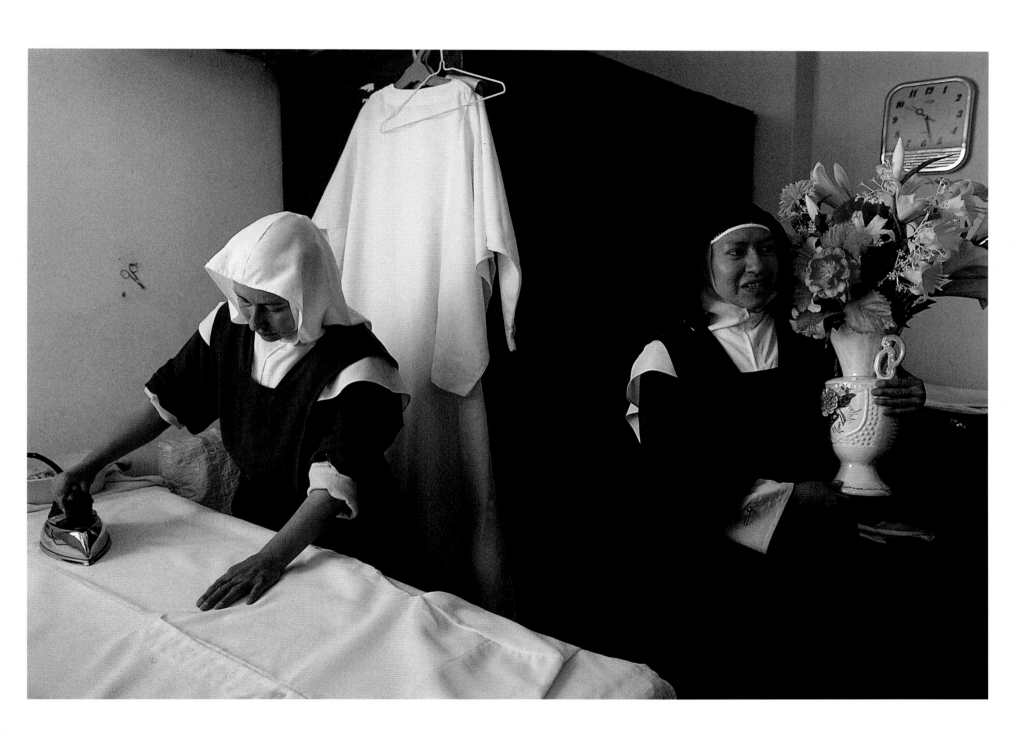

Sister Maria de Jesucristo irons habits; while Sister Raquel de
Santa Teresita arranges plastic flowers. Once accepted within
the convent, most sisters never again behold the outer world.

Cloistered Caremilite nuns at Carmen de la Asuncion, in Cuenca, serve tea to Archbishop Alberto Luna Tobar. Monseñor Luna is a national leader who led efforts to rebuild area towns after disastrous floods and landslides in 1993.

Brother Alfredo Lluminquinga, 24, has lived only five years in La Merced convent. Pedrito Villafuerte, age 103, entered the monastery some 90 years ago.

The Roman Catholic faith, battle standard of the conquistadors, has so long permeated national life that it can hardly be omitted from any consideration of Ecuador's history. Two of the nation's greatest presidents, Gabriel Garcia Moreno and Eloy Alfaro, lost their lives partly because of strongly opposing views of the roles of church and state.

Celebrants leap through a bonfire blazing at Saraguro in southern Ecuador on the evening of the June San Pedro-San Pablo festival. This custom originated in Europe as a traditional expression of Midsummer's Eve madness. Carried by Spaniards to the new world, the ritual is still practiced in the Canary Islands, Potosí and La Paz in Bolivia, the Cordillera Blanca in Peru, and Otavalo in Ecuador.

In Azogues, Cañar Province, friends and family carry the casket
of María de Lourdes into church.

Daughters of María de Lourdes mourn during the funeral Mass.
Doña María sold fruit in the Azogues market.

A young girl and her sister tend the flock near Cuenca, where traditional life-styles are as unchanged as the mountainous terrain.

Watched by young Mateo García Game, their common nephew,
María José de Game feeds her cousin María Victoria
Altamirano. The infant's mother is in the hospital, giving
birth to one more citizen of Quito.

A young couple passes the time while waiting in Uyumbicho, on the Panamerican Highway south of Quito, for a beauty pageant to begin.

Clouds envelop slopes of the Candelaria region in Chimborazo
Province. Nearby El Altar was perhaps Ecuador's highest
mountain until it exploded a thousand years ago, leaving an
enormous crater. The eruption survives in local legend.

Near Barabón, in Azuay Province, a girl wearing a straw
"Panama" hat characteristic of the region enjoys a swing
while waiting for a milk truck to come.

Threshing grain in Zumbahua, Cotopaxi Province, is accomplished by driving a team of horses around and around. The straw will be saved to mix with mud for the manufacture of adobes needed to construct walls and buildings.

Bandmaster Luis Cevallos of San Pablo, a town overlooking the lake of the same name in Imbabura Province, sits among his certificates and memorabilia. Almost every community in Ecuador can produce a brass band with tireless drummers to provide the music and the beat essential for the proper celebration of civic events and festivals.

Ex-president Osvaldo Hurtado argues his points of view in a committee appointed by President Sixto Durán-Ballén to suggest reforms of the national constitution. After innumerable coups, several dictatorships, and at least a dozen constitutions, the army drew one up in 1978 granting universal suffrage. Since then, Ecuador has been extolled as one of the most democratic Latin-American nations.

In the northern city of
Ibarra, a boy enters the
inmates section of a prison
to join his mother. Children
who lack other support may
remain with their mothers
and move freely within
the building.

In Quito's San Patricio youth center, a school for homeless boy's directed by Salesian Fathers, children are educated by the "preventive system" of San Juan Bosco, a method based on reason, religion and kindness, as well as hard work.

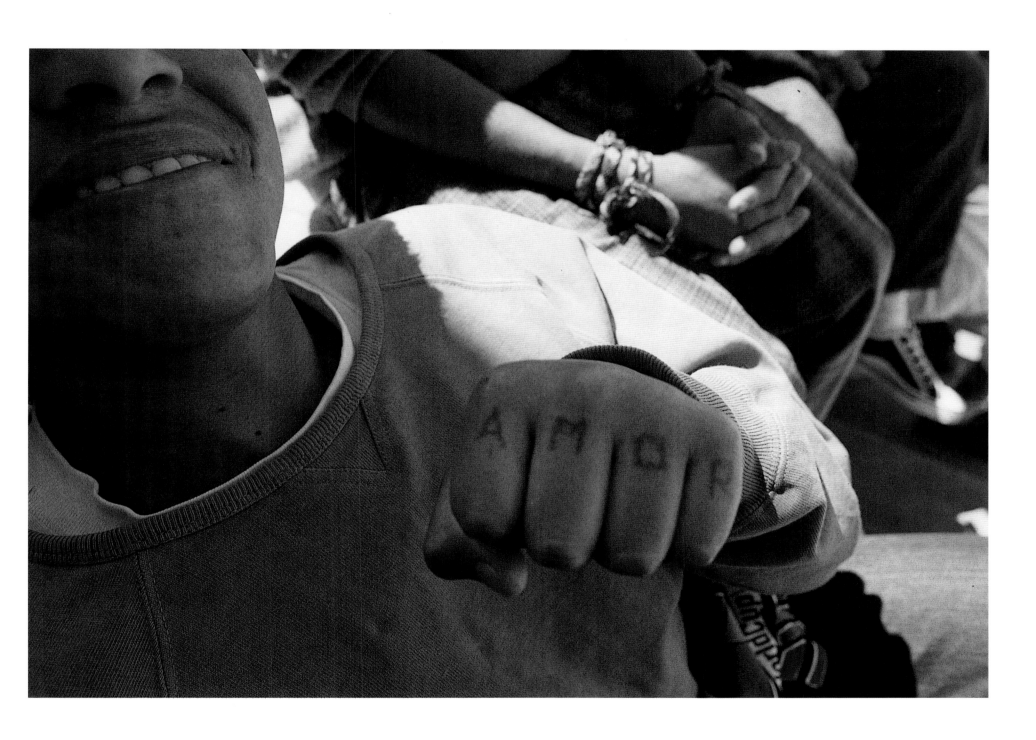

The Italian order of Salesians is known throughout the Latin world for manual training and teaching of self-sufficiency to youths. Their schools, clubs, and camps are welcome in Ecuador where 40 percent of the population is less than 15 years old.

Unique among native Americans for their enterprise and social self-betterment, Otavalans manufacture and sell woven clothing throughout the Western world.

A band plays a local interpretation of "La Virgin de la Macarena" at a bullfight in Olmedo, northeast of Quito, at the edge of the Cayambe-Coca Ecological Reserve.

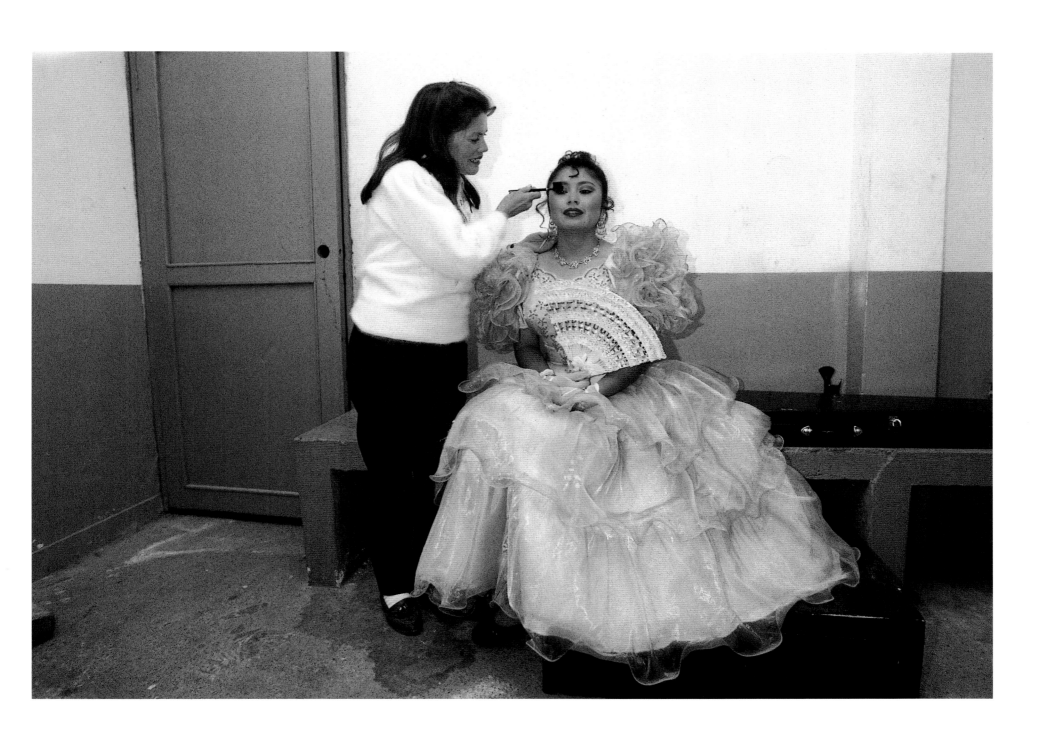

Jimena Custodio applies makeup to María Angel who aspires to
be the beauty queen of Uyumbicho, a town south of Quito.

Only a few minutes drive north of the equator, Tabacundo is a bucolic community brimming with ancient history. The nearby Cochasquí pyramids, built by Caranqui Indians in the twelfth or thirteenth century, were probably astronomical observatories that verified dates of religious and funerary rites.

Morning fog lifts from the chill waters of Lake San Pablo to reveal Mount Imbabura in the province of the same name. The lake lies in farmlands north of the equator but close enough to Quito to invite considerable tourist traffic. A marathon swim every September attracts contestants from all over the republic who have trained hard for the breathtaking event.

Professional mountain climber Rómulo Cárdenas tests the southern slopes of Cayambe, the preferred route to the 18,996-foot summit. At about the 16,000-foot level Rómulo will cross the equator at the only place on earth where the invisible line is drawn through ice and snow. The northern side of Cayambe, of almost vertical volcanic rock given to crumbling, is too dangerous to climb without risk of a horrifying fall.

EL ORIENTE

The Rain Forest

Warm mist fogs the shore of Laguna Grande in the Cuyabeno Wildlife Reserve. The vast plain of Amazonia tilts so imperceptibly from the Andes towards the Atlantic Ocean that waters seeking outlet to the sea meander and inundate the land much of the year. In the largely liquid ecosystem birds and fish prosper if let alone.

Mauricio Mendua, an aging elder of the Cofan tribe, is flanked by the enormous buttresses of a ceiba tree as he searches the banks of the Aguarico River for certain palm fronds needed to thatch his house in the forest. Cofan elders cling to knowledge of rain-forest plants acquired through the centuries of usage; younger tribes people attracted by western ways show less interest in such traditional values.

The Rio Reventador is one of hundreds that drain the highlands into the larger rivers of Amazonia. In the course of their descent, the streams saturate slopes that range from polar to tropical, creating countless "micro climates" and habitats that harbor an astounding range of species.

Despite its limited territorial scope, Ecuador contains at least three thousand species of wild orchids, some 10 percent of the world total. Most of them grow in the cloud forests on either the eastern or the western slopes of the Cordillera of the Andes. The variety of flora and fauna has led some scientists to deem the country a region of "biological megadiversity."

The tropical rain-forest system is upside down, compared to temperate forests; its nutrients are stored not so much in the soil as overhead. Many creatures live their entire lives in the canopy without touching earth. To escape predators, some insects are disguised in deceptive shapes and coloring that imitates leaves, branches, or fiercer forms of life.

Most of the entrails of the tropical rain forests—particularly the life forms of the high canopy, unseen both from the ground and from the air—still await discovery. All species, of whatever shape or color, are thought to be interrelated in some way or another. Many have been catalogued but only a few species have been examined in enough detail to determine their possible roles with regard to other species, including humankind.

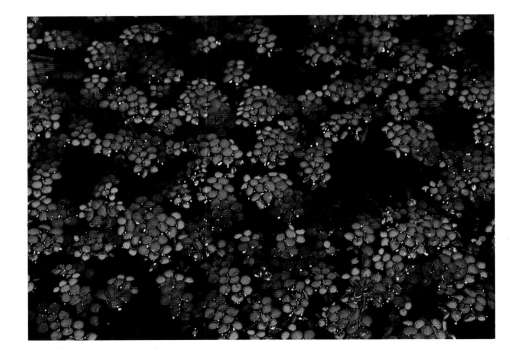

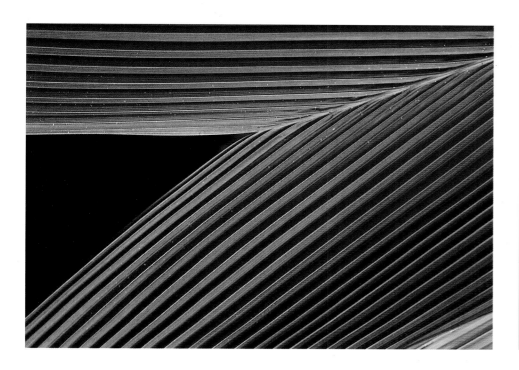

Mariana Samik of the Shuar community of Asunción gets ready to prepare a midday meal in her relatively modern home built of sawed lumber. In centuries past, both the Incas and the Spaniards avoided her ancestors, whose warlike zeal inspired fear. In recent times, the oil industry has invaded Shuar lands and Mariana's people are now actively involved in organizing indigenous communities and defending their forest environment.

Broken glass reflects the visage of a headman of the Achuar community near the Conambo River in the vast Pastaza Province of southeastern Ecuador. His ceremonial headdress and body paint are characteristic of ritual adornment common to all Amazonians prior to change brought by the European conquest. The paint is a vegetable dye, achiote in Spanish and urucú in Brazil; annatto when used for modern lipstick and food coloring. Feathers plucked from the bodies of countless birds, mostly toucans, are fashioned into the elaborate headdresses which today command lofty prices when they enter the tourist souvenir trade.

Heart of palm is the delicacy shared by Octavio Lucitante and Silverio Crillo in the clearing they have slashed from the forest near Zábalo in the northern Oriente (*above*). A transAndean pipeline (*right*) carries petroleum from wells in the northern Oriente to national refineries, and to the world from the Altlantic seaport, Esmeraldas. In becoming Ecuador's main export product, oil has damaged the Oriente environment, not only directly through serious oil spills but also indirectly by spurring road building, lumbering, and uncontrolled colonization.

In the Oriente, a humming-bird (left) shot in flight with a poison blowgun dart demonstrates the incredible accuracy of an Achuar hunter. A yellow-eyed tiger heron (opposite) has become a pet in the home of a Siona headman. Wild creatures are often tamed by rain forest Indians, but fathers instruct their sons not to use the creatures for target practice. Ecuador has roughly 300 species of frogs, whereas the United States, a country 33 times larger, holds only 80 species in all its lakes and forests.

San Rafael waterfall leaps
from the slopes of 11,686-
foot El Reventador, an active
volcano rising from the cloud
forest. The 475-foot plunge
into the lowlands is the
greatest of any in Ecuador.

Life teems throughout the Oriente, whether in fallen tree trunks, beneath leaves, deep in the soil, under water, or high in the canopy. Scientists wonder about the source of such diversity. Some conjecture that equatorial zones became refuges of life forms when glaciers brought deadly cold to much of the earth's surface.

Of the forty-odd kinds of rain forests in Amazonia, only a few can survive tree roots being flooded part or all of the year. In Laguna Grande of the Cuyabeno Wildlife Reserve exist some species of palms, and other trees such as these Macrolobium, which have become adapted to long inundation. During times of flood, fish feed on fruits and nuts, crocodilians and reptiles live at the water's edge, and large aquatic mammals such as pink dolphins and manatees find ecological niches here. At the top of the Laguna Grande food chain are jaguars. They are the largest cats of the Americas and very strong swimmers.

ISLAS GALAPAGOS

Galapagos Islands

Upon first sighting a marine iguana in 1835, Charles Darwin described it as "a hideous-looking creature, of a dirty black colour, stupid, and sluggish in its movements." Stupid they may be, but marine iguanas have outlived many smarter creatures. They have managed to survive thousands of years of prehistoric past and will certainly continue to populate the rocky shores of Galapagos in large numbers well into the twenty-first century, now that most of the islands form a national park. Visitors often share Darwin's reaction; even scientists are astonished by the other-worldly nature of the islands.

Tips of huge shield volcanoes ejected from a fixed "hot spot" beneath the ocean floor, the islands appeared in recent geologic time, one to five million years ago. As the Nazca tectonic plate of the basaltic ocean floor carries them slowly to the southeast, newer islands in the northwest emerge from the surface of the sea and still erupt from time to time. Pinnacle Rock rises from Bartolomé Island (foreground).

On Punto Espinosa, Fernandina Island, a marine iguana winks at
a visitor. He can dive as deep as 40 feet into the cold sea to
feed on marine algae. After an hour or so he will crawl out into
the sun to warm his blood and increase his metabolism.

To rid themselves of the excess salt consumed under water,
marine iguanas expel it by means of special glands. On the lava
beaches they are usually accompanied by sally lightfoot crabs
which nourish themselves with the same organic detritus that
appeals to the iguanas.

The mating season for the male marine iguanas on Fernandina Island is announced by reddish and greenish changes in their otherwise black coloration. Their territorial imperatives are fought out in very slow motion.

Land iguanas, heavier than the marine species and a meter long, inhabit the desert parts of only six of the archipelago's 13 major islands. (There are six smaller islands and 42 islets). Their main diet is the spiny fruit of the Opuntía cactus. Six species of the cacti are unique, as with many other specialized life forms in Galapagos. The Opuntía grows an unusually long stem to lift its shoots above the reach of tortoises and iguanas here on Santa Fe Island.

A male frigate bird inflates his red throat pouch to football size to attract females during mating season.

Blue-footed boobies perform a mating dance. Visitors to the islands can easily see and photograph these intimate moments since the boobies on Daphne Mayor Island, like most Galapagos wildlife, pay no attention whatever to human observers. Either the male or the female—they are hard to distinguish—may pick up a stick or stone and deposit it with great ceremony in an imaginary nest.

Blue-footed boobies lay one to three eggs a year. To define the limits of the nest during the incubation period, this couple on Sombrero Chino Island will squirt guano in a circle around the nest to mark and eventually to elevate its rim so that fledglings are held inside.

Eggs of this blue-footed boobie on Sombrero Chino Island are
beginning to hatch. The mother will protect the nest.

This fledgling on Daphne Mayor Island will soon take off on its own. The mother goes fishing and regurgitates his catch to feed his young.

Marvelous flying machines with wingspreads of six or seven feet, frigate birds fly atop tropical oceans but never land on water because they lack oil glands to waterproof their feathers. They are amazingly adept at scooping food from the surface while flying at high speed. Because they are aggressive and piratical, often forcing lesser birds to drop food in flight so that it can be snatched from the air, they are traditionally called man-o'-war birds.

Masked boobies greet
tourists at Punta Suárez
on Española Island, the
southernmost point of land
in Galapagos.

At about 12 pounds weight,
the waved albatross is the
largest native Galapagos
bird. Twelve thousand pairs
exist, on Española Island
only.

A flightless cormorant spreads its vestigial wings. Since they were never bothered by predators on the coasts of Isabela and Fernandina Islands, their wings eventually shriveled.

Frigate birds following a cruise ship can easily be identified by
their size, their split tail, and their graceful, soaring flight.

Flamingoes sleep standing up in a lake near Cormorant Point on Floreana Island.

Galapagos vegetation is usually desert-like near the sea, becoming greener and thicker towards the summits of the larger islands which reach into wetter air. The palosanto trees (right), are evenly spaced to afford each one its share of scarce moisture.

Seals of Galapagos are playful and accustomed to humans. An unforgettable tourist experience on several islands is to be met by a school of sea lions upon entering a harbor and then to swim and play in crystalline waters with them. Sometimes a young one, swimming on its back, will glide right into a tourist's arms.

When sea lions, full of food, crawl out onto rocky shores and climb perhaps a hundred feet above the sea, they are hard to see, especially in the dark. To stumble on one at night, provoking it to rear and roar, can startle an intruder.

The *Galapagos* (meaning tortoise, among other things, in Spanish) gave their name to the Islands. Weighing as much as 600 pounds and living as long as 150 years, the tortoises long provided a lasting source of meat for sailing ships, since they could be turned upside down and kept alive for months. Some species have thus become extinct and others are few. The Charles Darwin Research Station on Santa Cruz Island sponsors conservation and reproduction of all surviving species of the giant tortoises.

The slow passage of a captive tortoise, which may live many
more years, is watched by a cow whose days are numbered.
Cattle are raised for local consumption on Santa Cruz, a
populated island.

Cattle are butchered at the slaughterhouse in Puerto Ayora, Santa Cruz Island. A traditional open air *camal*, one of the last in Ecuador, it will soon be replaced by a modern installation.

Santa Cruz workers unload cement at Puerto Ayora from one of the two ships a month that bring supplies.

Uniformed schoolgirls at Puerto Ayora's secondary school attend a dance at a going-away party for their teacher who is moving to Quito.

A parasol lessens the impact of the equatorial sun in Puerto Ayora. Since vehicles are few, paved roads aren't essential.

Las Encantadas, The Enchanted Isles, was the first name bestowed on the Galapagos by their discoverer, Tomás de Berlanger, Bishop of Panama. He was on his way to Peru in 1535 but strayed far west of his proper course. In the late seventeenth century buccaneers buried booty in the islands, and in the nineteenth, sealers savaged the wildlife. In 1841, novelist Herman Melville, author of *Moby Dick*, visited the islands and wrote an essay entitled Las Encantadas. Darwin helped make them famous but for three centuries after their discovery no one claimed The Enchanted Isles, one of the world's richest wildlife preserves.

LA COSTA

The Coast

Bounty of the azure sea, twelve tons of carduma shine like silver on the sun-lit beach of Cabuyal in Esmeraldas Province. A huge sailing raft was captured off this coast in 1526 by a vessel Francisco Pizarro sent to confirm the existence of the Inca Empire. The raft's cargo included woolens with animal designs woven in color and mirrors of burnished silver. The Spaniards seized some of the raft's passengers to teach them to become interpreters for the coming Conquest.

On the same day as this soccer game on the beach near San Miguel, the World Cup finals reigned in the United States. For a billion fans little else on earth was worthy of such rapt attention.

Bedecked with flowers and draped with ribbons, the little church of Puerto Hualtaco, in El Oro Province, is ready for an evening of three baptisms and a wedding ceremony. Religion plays a large role in domestic life, although anti-clerical leaders from the Coast drove the church out of government and education in the first decade of the century. Earlier, Ecuador had been a theocracy where only practicing Roman Catholics could vote.

In the heat and humidity of Borbón, a town in Esmeraldas province, juicy slices of watermelon tempt passersby. This lumber town on the banks of the Cayapas River has recently grown to more than 7,000 inhabitants while the native forest, on which it depends, has shrunk to four percent of its original acreage.

A lunch of lentils, rice, and fish, the basic diet of many Costeños,
satisfies Teresa Quiñones. Many citizens of African descent
have moved into the Borbón area to cut trees and build homes,
thus provoking outrage among the Chachis, descendants of the
aboriginal inhabitants of lands along the Cayapas River.

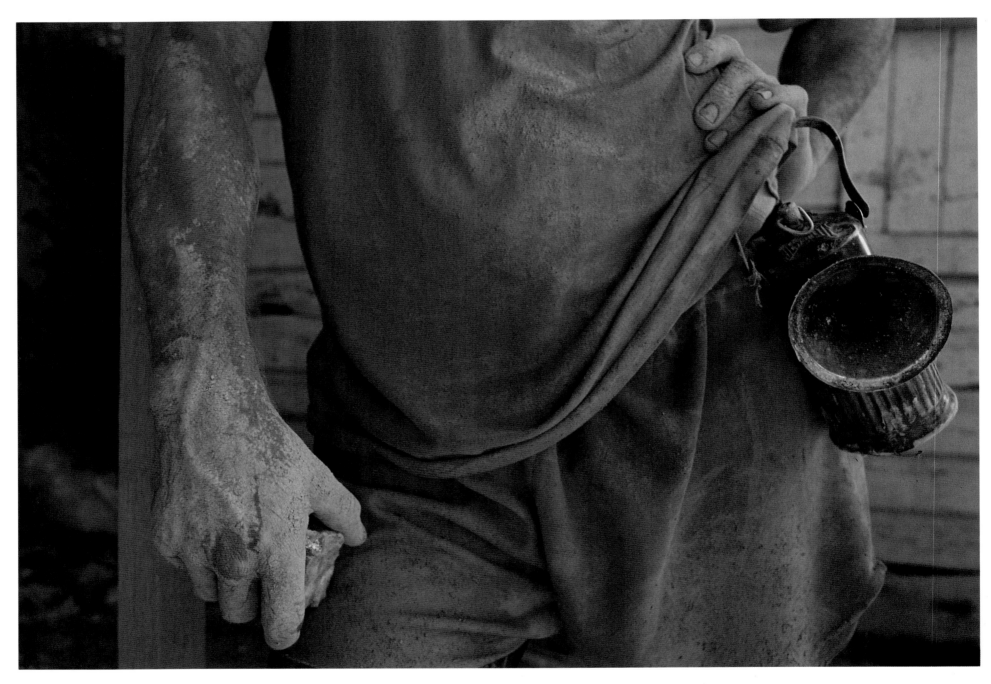

Since extracting gold from the aptly-named province of El Oro affords miner Servio Ramirez of Zaruma a salary well above the national average, he doesn't plan to quit "unless I'm flattened by a cave-in." In the sixteenth century, gold lured Spaniards to Zaruma, where the landscape is still dotted with crumbling wooden houses and empty mine shafts reminiscent of a rich but painful colonial past.

The fair complexion of Mariuxi Salto of Cañitas, Manabí Province, suggests a lineage characteristic of many citizens of the Coast. Their ancestors were often largely European and African, with fewer of the aboriginal race that predominates in the rural Sierra.

Of the 100,000 inhabitants of Esmeraldas, the principal northern seaport, most are of African descent. As elsewhere in the Americas, their ancestors were imported to work in plantations after the Indians—who never accepted slavery—ran away, died of despair or lowland tropical diseases or were freed by royal decree. Ecuadorian slaves were emancipated in 1851, but their descendants still crowd the lower end of the economic scale.

A supper is being prepared for María Quiñonez (left) in a restaurant of Esmeraldas, a city where Christianity sometimes gets mixed with spiritism of African origins.

The parents of Liliana and Fernanda (above) own a restaurant in Cañitas, Manabí Province. The girls, far less timid than most highlanders of the same age, help in the restaurant when not in school.

At the Esmeraldas bus station, a ranchera will render a well-ventilated ride when it picks up speed. Passengers in the heart of the torrid zone are always thankful for a breeze.

High jumper Fernando Pincay came to Guayaquil a year ago to look for work, as with many of his rural friends who seek their fortunes in the big city. They live in the wooden shacks of Trinidad Island (background), one of the new towns of the sprawling metropolis.

Petroleum from the Oriente flows through a valve opened by Angel Guerrero at the state oil refinery in Esmeraldas.

A capuchin monkey whose natural home is in the high canopy of the rain forest looks over a catch of fish—for which he has no appetite—at the edge of the Cayapas River in Esmeraldas Province.

The best Panama hats were made in Montecristi. Old men weave them in the first light of day, when humidity is high and the straw is supple. Panama hats were styled by Roosevelt's Rough Riders and celebrities such as Napoleon III, Al Capone, Charley Chan, and Fitzcarraldo of Amazon operatic fame. Co-owner of this hat factory and warehouse is Juana Vicente Alova.

Once the nation's principal export at 5,000,000 units a year, Panama hats fell out of favor after World War II. Despite the disastrous decline, Rosa Delgada still sells both cheap and exquisite models at prices ranging from one to fifty dollars.

As if in remembrance of times past, a three-masted sailing ship is moored by Guayaquil's old city hall on the waterfront of the nation's largest and fastest growing city. As part of their preparation to defend Ecuador and represent the nation abroad, naval academy cadets (above) embark on the school ship *Guayas* for round-the-world training cruises and good-will missions.

In 1867 a great fire burned down Babahoyo, Los Rios Province, then a highly combustible city built of wood and cane. It was rebuilt, and is now home to 51,000 people who live on a tributary of the Guayas River well inland from the coast. While men work in banana plantations and mothers find employment in town, grandmothers mind the children.

Live marimba music fills the air at Bellavista, in Esmeraldas
Province. Blasina Ayovi Camacho beats the tom-tom.

Patrons of a Guayaquil tavern sing the nostalgic folk music
popularized throughout Latin America by Ecuadorian singer
Julio Jaramillo.

The marimba, the rhythmic heart of popular music in Esmeraldas, came to the Americas with the slave trade. Originating in Java, it wandered across Africa centuries ago, preserving the original Javanese musical scales. Along Ecuador's northern coast the marimba is usually hung from the ceiling and sometimes played on opposite sides by two people. Lizardo Valencia, who lives near the Onzole River, uses iron-hard chonta palm wood for the keys and splits natural tubes of guadua bamboo for the resonators placed under the keys.

Fifty centuries ago fisherfolk
founded a civilization near
this beach. Ceramics of the
Valdivia culture are among
the oldest ever discovered
in the Western Hemisphere.
Some archaeologists
contend that people have
dwelt in Valdivia village,
Guayas Province, at least
two millennia.

A family store in Charapotó,
Manabí Province, can supply
almost any neighborhood
need: food, clothing, hard-
ware, farm utensils, auto
parts and outboard motors.

Wrapping his arms around
the new and the old, Doctor
Manuel Eduardo Andrade of
Portoviejo, Manabí Province,
poses with his daughter and
a portrait of a famous fore-
father. General Eloy Alfaro
was a powerful president of
Ecuador early in the century.

Representing liberal and
business interests centered
in Guayaquil, he achieved the
separation of church and
state and construction of
the spectacular Guayaquil-
Quito railroad.

Interior designer Tanya Klein de Palacios chats with her
daughter Arianna Mandini in the kitchen of her home in
Guayaquil. Both mother and daughter have won the title
Miss Ecuador.

Beauty queen Arianna Mandini, who is active in community
affairs, jokes with her younger sister in her Guayaquil home.

Santano Valdez harvests rice in his fields near Roca-fuerte, in the Manabí province. The coastal rainy season, between December and June, provides an appropriate environment for the growing of rice, which is one of Ecuador's main food staples.

Harvesting rice in Manabí Province calls on the talents of the entire Rivadeneira family. After the paddies are dried out, children join their parents in cutting, carrying and threshing the sheaves.

While spreading rice to dry under the sun, Segundo Mera is distracted by his son Andres. Meanwhile, one of Segundo's chickens gorges unseen on a bountiful meal.

Bound for foreign ports, boxes of green bananas are loaded into the hold of a cargo ship by Guayaquil stevedores. As the world's largest exporter of bananas, Ecuador has an economy distressingly dependent upon other nations' import restrictions, taxes and price controls placed on a perishable product.

Cockfighting is called a sport, but it is really a gambling game in
Colón, Manabí Province.

One tax-free enterprise is giving a pedicure to a friend in
Borbón, Esmeraldas Province.

Principal fluvial artery of
Ecuador, the Guayas River
drains one of the wealthiest
regions of South America
and provides the nation with
an abundance of crops, many
of them for export: bananas,
cotton, rice, cacao, coffee,
sugar, corn, peanuts, soy
and tobacco.

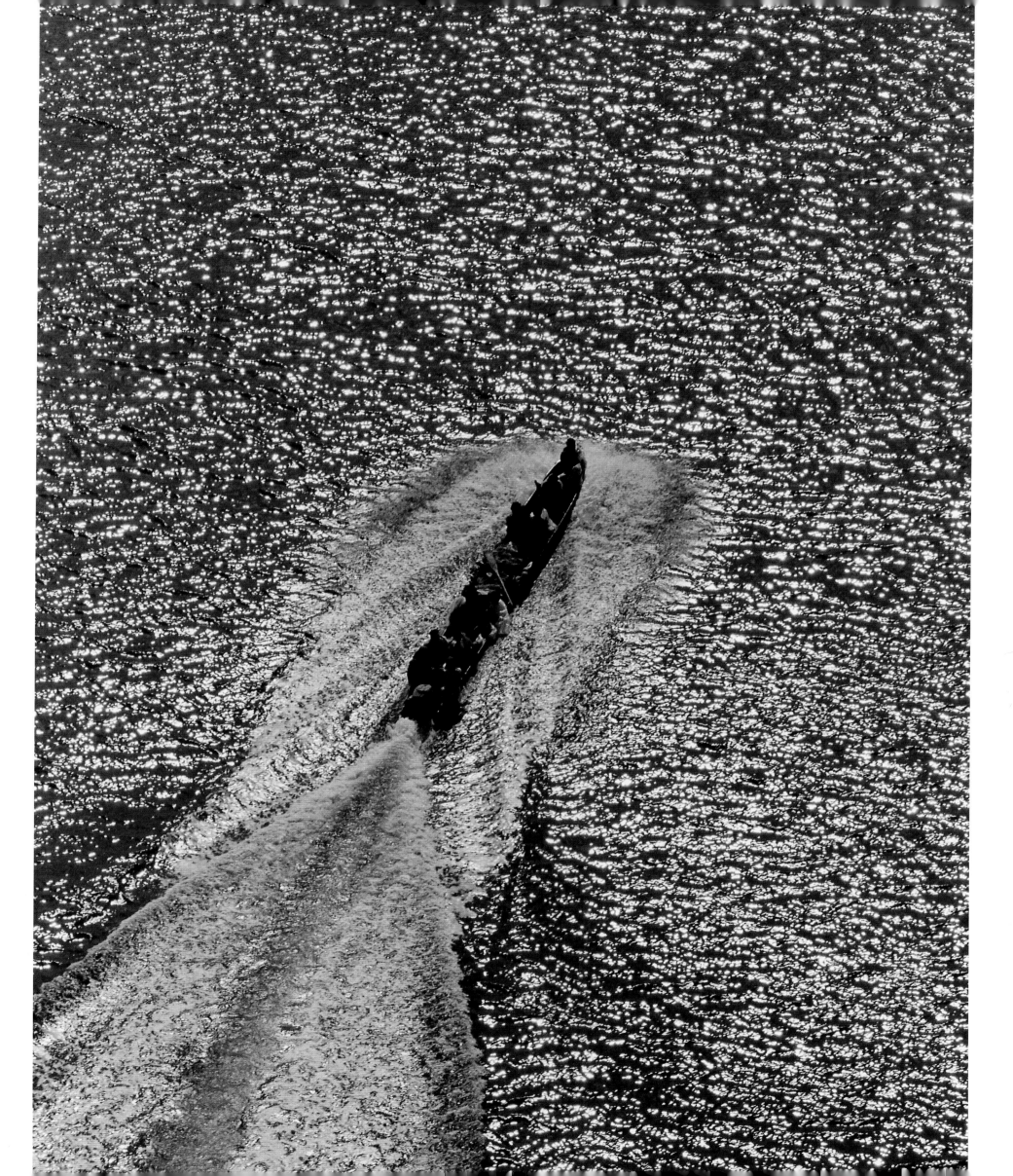

Swapping glances in a Borbón restaurant, Teodoro José Arroyo
Ponce and Herminia Jaramillo Preciado represent the open and
mobile relationships of young people on the Coast.

Among the mangroves of Salinas, Manabí, Charito puffs on a
cigar to ward off mosquitoes. When crab fishermen go into the
mangroves, they carry smoking torches to keep the bugs at bay.

One of the finest watering places in Ecuador is Playas, on the Gulf of Guayaquil, where the shrimp fleet anchors at sundown. While Ecuador's cities fill with distractions, the ocean remains unchanged and its horizons beckon as one grows up. This lad's father followed the sea; he, too, may set forth someday.

Credits

Biographies

PHOTOGRAPHERS AND EDITORS
TOUR THE GALAPAGOS ISLANDS.

François Ancellet (France)
is a freelance photographer for the French picture agency Rapho Photography. Photographs from his work in the Brazilian and Ecuadorian rainforests appear in the book, "Mundos Amazonicos."

Jorge Juan Anhalzer (Ecuador)
is a self-taught freelance photographer and mountaineering/adventure guide. He is the author of several photographic books including "Tierras Altas," "Parques Nacionales del Ecuador," "100 Imagenes del Ecuador," and "Ecuador Desde el Aire."

Mariana Bazo (Peru)
is the Reuters staff photographer for the Lima bureau. Many of her photographs documenting the political violence in Peru have been published world-wide. Bazo was also the 1993-94 Reuters Willie Vicoy Fellow at the University of Missouri School of Journalism.

Alan Berner (United States)
has degrees in philosophy and photojournalism from the University of Missouri. A staff photographer at the *Seattle Times* for 12 years, Berner

CÉSAR AND BOLO FRANCO IN THE
GALAPAGOS ISLANDS.

has covered many social issue stories, including Washington's American Indian tribes, Seattle's homeless and pollution. He's worked on a number of book projects including "A Day in the Life of America," "A Day in the Life of California," and "Power to Heal." He has also been the National Press Photographer's Association's Regional Press Photographer of the Year three times and runner-up five times.

Yann Arthus-Bertrand (France)
is an international photographer and founder of the picture agency, Altitude, specializing in aerial photography. Arthus-Bertrand's work has been published in *Life*, *National Geographic*, *Elle*, *Paris Match*, *Figaro*, *Airone*, *Stern*, and *Geo* as well as several other major magazines. He is the author of more than 30 books.

James Blair (United States)
recently retired from the *National Geographic* after more than 30 years as a staff photographer for the magazine. During that time he had 48 stories published. One of his major articles, in June 1977, was on South Africa. As a result of this coverage, he was made a Poynter Fellow for one of the Yale Seminars in Modern Journalism. He also received the Overseas Press Club of America Award for Best Photographic Reporting from Abroad in 1977 for his coverage of South Africa.

Alberto Borbón (Costa Rica)
who specializes in nature photography, has had work included in exhibits in Costa Rica and Mexico. He is currently working on a project supporting the protection of the environment in Costa Rica.

Aldo Brando (Colombia)
is a freelance photographer who specializes in nature and underwater photography. His photos have been published in numerous books, including "Colombia from the Air and Malpelo."

Judy Bustamante (Ecuador)
is a freelance photographer whose photographs have appeared in *Geo*, *the New York Times*, *Travel*, *Americas*, and *Diners* magazines. She has also worked as a photo and news editor for the Ecuadorian newspaper, *El Comercio*. She won First Prize in the National Photography Competition organized by the Superintendent of Banks of Ecuador, 1986; First Prize Premio PRISMA for Excellence in Advertising sponsored by Dinediciones, 1990, and Third Prize in the international photography contest, "Emancipation and Identity of Latin America 1492-1992 in 1990.

Fabián Cevallos (France)
is a freelance photographer specializing in portraiture and cinema photography. He is of Otavalan Indian descent, but has spent the majority of his life in France and Italy. He has worked with such cinematic luminaries as Bertolucci, Pasolini, Visconti, Coppola and Fellini. His work has appeared in *Life*, *Stern*, *Time*, *Panorama* and *Paris Match* magazines.

Diego Cifuentes (Ecuador)
is a freelance photographer. His photographs have been exhibited throughout Western Europe and Latin America, and he has two books, "500 anos de que?" and "Canto a la Realidad: Lo mejor de la Fotografia Latinoamericana 1860-1993," to his credit. His photographs have also appeared in *Diners* magazine, the newspapers *Hoy* and *El Comercio* and in the magazine for the Institute of Human Rights.

Jan Colbert (United States)
is an assistant professor at the University of Missouri School of Journalism where she teaches magazine design and writing. She is the managing editor and art director for two magazines, *The IRE Journal* and the *National Book Critics Circle Journal*. She is the co-editor of "The Reporter's Handbook," published by St. Martin's Press, and she is currently writing a book on in-depth reporting, writing and photography methods.

Pablo Corral (Ecuador)
is a freelance photographer and editor. He is the author of three photographic books, "Bare Earth;" "Silent Landscapes: The Andes of Ecuador," and "Ecuador, from Magic to Horror." In addition to directing the *Descubriendo Ecuador* project, Corral is coordinating a major photographic project for the Latin American Confederation of Graphic Industries. He also holds a doctoral degree in law and political science from the Catholic University in Quito.

Mike Davis (United States)
is an illustrations editor at *National Geographic Magazine*. Before joining the *Geographic* he was picture editor for the Albuquerque (N.M.) *Tribune*. While at the *Tribune* Davis was named the Picture Editor of the Year (1990) in the Pictures of the Year competition and National Press Photographer's Association's Clip Contest Picture Editor of the Year (1989). A master's degree recipient from

the University of Missouri School of Journalism, Davis has also been a picture editor on three books: "The Power to Heal;" "A Day in the Life of Italy," and "10,000 Eyes." And, he was a jury member for the W. Eugene Smith Fellowship.

Peter Essick (United States)
is a freelance photojournalist based in Brooklyn, New York. He is a frequent contributor to *National Geographic*. His work has also been published in *Geo*, *The New York Times Magazine* and many other major publications. He has twice been runner-up as the Magazine Photographer of the Year in the Pictures of the Year competition. He received his master's degree from the University of Missouri School of Journalism.

Melissa Farlow (United States)
a freelance photographer based in Pittsburgh, has worked primarily as a newspaper staff photographer. While working for the *Louisville Courier Journal* she was a member of the photographic staff that won the Pulitzer Prize in 1975 for their coverage of desegregation of the public school system. Farlow's first story for *National Geographic* was on the Okefenokee Swamp. She also contributed to a *National Geographic* story on Northern California, and with her husband, Randy Olson, has recently completed a story on issues facing the national parks of the United States. She was twice a finalist for the W. Eugene Smith grant for humanistic photography.

Denis Finley (United States)
is an award-winning picture editor and photographer for the *Virginian-Pilot*. In addition he has worked as a photography intern with the *National Geographic*. Finley was National College Photographer of the Year in 1987. He received his master's degree from the University of Missouri School of Journalism.

Bolo Franco (Ecuador)
is a freelance photographer. His work has appeared in the book, "Inside Guide-Ecuador," as well as on many postcards and posters. He also has contributed to a book currently being edited about the Ecuadorian coast. It will be published by the Cultural Promotion Department of the Central Bank of Ecuador.

Cesar Franco (Ecuador)
is a freelance photographer. His photographs have appeared on many postcards and posters as well as in the book, "Inside Guide-Ecuador." Franco has also contributed to a book about the

Ecuadorian coast to be published by the Cultural Promotion Department of the Central Bank of Ecuador. He studied photography at Colorado College and at the Academy of Art in San Francisco, California.

Marcela García (Ecuador)
is a freelance photographer. Her photographs have been exhibited in various cities throughout Ecuador as well as in Brazil and Italy. Garcia was also a contributor to the exposition *Images of Silence* in the late 1980s. This collection of photographs from Latin America and the Caribbean was exhibited at the Museum of Modern Art of Latin America in the Organization of American States building, Washington, D.C.

Kate Glassner Brainerd (United States)
as the owner and director of KGB Partnership in Denver, Colorado, works with photographers to edit and design books, personal projects and self-promotional material. Prior to creating KGB Partnership, Glassner Brainerd worked as an editor and designer at several newspapers and as a layout editor for the *National Geographic*. She has more than eight published books to her credit.

Santiago Harker (Colombia)
a freelance photographer, has been working exclusively in travel photography since 1983 and is the author of the book, "Colombia Inedita." In 1988 Harker received a grant from the Colombian Cultural Institute to complete a photographic essay on Colombia's national parks. In addition to Colombia, his work has been exhibited and published in Venezuela, Mexico, Iceland, Switzerland and Italy.

Jeremy Horner (England)
is a freelance photographer who has shot photographs in more than 50 countries. Since 1991 he has been working for UNICEF and has specialized in Latin America. His work has appeared in *Travel and Leisure*, the London *Times* and in *Odyssey Guides*. He is the author of the book, "The Life of Colombia."

Michio Hoshino (Japan)
one of Japan's most renowned photographers, specializes in nature and wildlife photography. His work has appeared in *National Geographic*, *Geo* and *Audubon* magazines. Hoshino has also published books about Alaska, grizzly bears, caribou and the Arctic.

Kent Kobersteen (United States)
has been associate director of photography at *National Geographic* Magazine since 1991. He joined the *National Geographic* in 1983 as an illustrations editor. In 1987 he became assistant director of photography. Before joining the *National Geographic*, Kobersteen spent eighteen years at the Minneapolis *Tribune* where he won numerous awards for his photography. A series on global poverty, another on the drought in Africa's Sahel, and a third on the major oil-producing nations each received recognition from groups such as the Overseas Press Club and the National Press Photographers Association. He has participated, as a photographer and an editor, on various "A Day in the Life" book projects, including those on Australia, Hawaii, Japan, Canada and the Soviet Union. And, he is co-director of the International Photojournalism Workshops, which has conducted photography workshops in Bulgaria and Hungary.

Loup Langton (United States)
teaches photojournalism at the University of Missouri School of Journalism. In addition to

THE CAPTAIN OF THE AMBASSADOR I, KENT KOBERSTEEN AND PABLO CORRAL.

LOUP LANGTON IN OTAVALO.

DANIELE PELLIGRINI

directing the *Descubriendo Ecuador* project, Langton taught photography at Ecuador's Universidad San Francisco and conducted a photography workshop for professionals in Quito during the summer of 1993. He was also a speaker and panel member at the 1994 Bulgarian Visual Communications Conference in Sofia. As a freelance photographer, Langton was a contributor to the "Homeless in America" book in 1987, and he has photographed for *Newsweek*, *Photo* Magazine (France), *Focus*, *New York Newsday* and others. He is presently finishing his dissertation for a Ph.D. degree from the University of Texas.

Pascal Maitre (France)

has devoted much of his career to photographing life in Africa. He worked as a reporter and photographer for four years at *Jeune Afrique* Magazine, and he organized a photographic exhibit about Africa for UNESCO in 1986. His photographs have appeared in *Le Figaro*, *L'Express*, *Newsweek*, *Geo* (Germany), *Stern*, *Der Spiegel*, *Airone*, *Time*, *Life* and others. His photo exhibitions have included, *Syria: City Images*, *African Celebrations* and *The Land of Islam*.

PABLO CORRAL

Maitre was also a contributor to "A Day in the Life of America" and the author of the books, "Le Rwanda," "Barcelone" and "Le Zaire."

Michele McDonald (United States)

has been a staff photographer for the *Boston Globe* since 1989. Before that she was a photojournalist for the *Virginian-Pilot* and the Concord *Monitor*. Her work on black infant mortality tied for First Place from the National Association of Black Journalists and won runner-up for the Robert F. Kennedy award.

Loren McIntyre (United States)

is an author and photographer who took his first pictures of South America in 1935. His name appears on maps and in the "Guinness Book of World Records" (for his discovery of the ultimate source of the Amazon River), as well as hundreds of books and magazines that carry pictures or text concerning South America. McIntyre has written and illustrated several books on South American themes; one, "The Incredible Incas," 1975, has sold more than half a million copies and is still in print. McIntyre has also produced films in many countries and has been decorated three times by South American governments.

Robert Mertens (United States)

is an art and nature photographer who is interested in human spirituality and evolution as expressed visually in both ancient and modern art. He received his master of fine arts degree from the University of Hawaii and is represented by Photonica in New York and Image Finders in Vancouver for stock photography.

Randy Olson (United States)

is a freelance magazine photographer based in Pittsburgh, Pennsylvania. Olson was a staff photographer at the *Pittsburgh Press* for seven years and was named the National Newspaper Photographer of the Year in 1992 and runner up in 1990. Olson also received the Robert F. Kennedy Award for photojournalism in 1991. Olson has been published in *National Geographic*, *Fortune*, *Life*, *U.S. News & World Report* and has contributed to the "Day in the Life" books series in China, Italy, California and Ireland.

Daniele Pellegrini (Italy)

is a staff photographer for the Italian magazine, *Airone*. He is listed in the "Guinness Book of World Records" for having driven a truck across five continents during a two-and-a-half-year period.

Lello Piazza (Italy)

is the photo editor for *Airone*, an Italian magazine that features photographic stories about wildlife and culture. Piazza is also a professor of statistics at the Polytechnic University of Milan.

Peter Pfersick (United States)

teaches photography at the University of California Berkeley. He received his bachelor's degree from the University of Arizona in Psychology and a Master's in photography from Lone Mountain College. In 1971 he opened a camera/darkroom store and began his photographic teaching activities. Pfersick has exhibited in Mexico, Guatemala, Taiwan and Hungary and has given lectures in England, Ecuador, Hong Kong and India. He has also photographed in Czechoslovakia, Nepal, Poland, Brazil and Romania.

Susie Post (United States)

is a freelance photojournalist based in Pittsburgh, Pennsylvania. Much of her work has focused on humanitarian issues, both in the United States and internationally. Currently she is working on a story for the *National Geographic*. She works for Black Star picture agency of New York, and her clients have included *Newsweek*, *Forbes*, the *Philadelphia Inquirer* and *World Vision*. Before freelancing, Post worked as a staff photographer at the Pittsburgh *Press*. Among several other photographic awards Post has won the Robert F. Kennedy Award for Coverage of the Disadvantaged.

Eduardo Quintana (Ecuador)

a freelance photographer, created and coordinated the photographic exhibitions *Ecuador Tierra Dentro*, *Oye Fotero Tomame Una Foto*, and *Los Pata Salada*, shown in Ecuador, Peru and Germany as well as *La Danza* which appeared in Ecuador and Peru. Quintana was also the coordinator of the first national exhibit of nude photographs in Ecuador. He is the founder and director of the workshop, *Nuevodia* and a documentary photographer of the theatrical-arts.

Raghu Rai (India)

is one of India's most distinguished photographers. He works for the Magnum picture agency and is a frequent contributor to *Geo*, *National Geographic*, *Life*, *Paris Match*, the *New York Times Magazine* and *Newsweek*. In addition to having exhibited and received awards for his work both nationally and internationally, Rai has 25 of his photographs in the permanent collection of the Bibliotheque Nationale in Paris. He is also the author of several books including "Mother Theresa," "Delhi: A Portrait," "The Sikhs," "Indira Gandhi," "Taj Mahal" and "Dreams of India."

Sylvie Rebbot (France)

is the picture editor for *Geo*, France. She has worked for several photo agencies including Sygma, Magnum and Odyssey and has collaborated on several books as an editor and advisor. Rebbot has also served as a jury member for many competitions, including one of France's most prestigious, the *Prix Niepce*. In addition, she is the current president of World Press Photo.

David Rees (United States)

teaches photojournalism at the University of Missouri and has been director of the College Photographer of the Year competition since 1987. He has served as lecturer and contest judge for professional photojournalism and design organizations throughout the midwest and actively freelances photos and stories to clients that have included: *Fortune*, *Farm Journal*, *Harrowsmith Magazine*, "World Book Encyclopedia," *USA Today* and the *Los Angeles Times*. He has one book to his credit, a photo book on the University of Missouri.

Guido Alberto Rossi (Italy)

created the picture agency, Action Press in Milan and assumed control of the stock agency, Image Bank, which now has offices in Milan, Rome and Modena. Rossi, a freelance photographer, is the author of 25 photographic books.

Kathy Ryan (United States)

photo editor of the *New York Times Magazine*, began her career at Sygma Photo Agency in 1978 and joined the *Times* in 1985 as deputy photo editor. Under her direction the magazine has won numerous photography awards, including Gold Medals from the Art Directors Club, the Society of Publication Designers and the Society of Newspaper Design. For the second year in a row she won First Place for overall Picture Editing in the Pictures of the Year competition. Ryan has taught at several workshops, including the Eddie Adams Workshop in 1991, '92 and '93, and the Santa Fe Workshop in 1992. She also conducted a photo editing workshop at Clarin newspaper in Buenos Aires in 1993. She is a member of the executive committee of the W. Eugene Smith Memorial Fund. And, she is currently editing a book titled: "Feeling the Spirit: The Family of Africa," photographed by Chester Higgins, Jr.

Diego Samper (Colombia)

is a freelance photographer, anthropologist, painter and writer. He has spent a number of years living in the Apaporis and Caqueta regions of the Amazon rainforest. Samper is also the co-author of several photographic books that pay homage to the natural beauty, architecture and cultural traditions of Colombia.

Byron Scott (United States)

is Meredith Professor of Magazine Journalism at the University of Missouri. A veteran of 21 years in teaching and 14 years in full-time journalism he has worked as a newspaper reporter, magazine editor and researcher in Miami, Chicago, Washington, D.C., New York and Los Angeles. From July 1992 to December 1993 he was in Bulgaria establishing the first American-style journalism program in Eastern Europe at the new American University in Blagoevgrad. He holds the first endowed chair in the history of the University of Missouri School of Journalism.

Paula Simas (Brazil)

works for the Brazilian magazine *Estoe*. She recently received international recognition for her photographic work detailing the lives of Brazil's street children.

Scott Thode (United States)

is a freelance photographer whose photographs have appeared in the *New York Times Magazine*, *Life*, *Newsweek*, *Geo* and several other North American and European publications. His work has been exhibited at the *Visa Pour L'Image* photo festival in Perpignon, France and in the *Electric Blanket* AIDS project, New York. In 1992 Thode was a finalist for the W. Eugene Smith Memorial Grant, won a first place at the Pictures of the Year competition sponsored by the University of Missouri School of Journalism and the NPPA and took second place at the Gordon Parks Commemorative Photography competition. He is currently finishing work on his book, "The Spirit Within," a series of portraits and writings of people who have AIDS or are HIV positive.

Matteo Torri (Ecuador)

a freelance photographer, began his career in his native country of Italy where he studied with various portrait and fashion photographers. Torri has received numerous international awards for his work, including the Kodak Prize for 1979 in Milan, the International Advertising

MICHELE MCDONALD AND SUSIE POST

Festival Award in 1990 and 1991 in New York, the Prisma Prize from *Diners* magazine in Quito and the C. Mantilla Prize from the Ecuadorian newspaper, *El Comercio*.

Carmen Troesser (United States)

recently finished her master's degree in photojournalism at the University of Missouri. She has been an intern at various newspapers throughout the United States and has won two international awards for her photo-illustrations in the Pictures of the Year competition. She has an art photography background.

Francisco Valdivieso (Ecuador)

is the general manager of Imprenta Mariscal in Quito. Valdivieso served as president of the Latin American Confederation of Graphic Industries (CONLATINGRAF) from 1989 to 1991. In 1992 he was awarded the title *America's Man of the Year* from the Printing Association of Florida. In addition, Valdivieso has many years of experience in photography, editing and design.

RAGHU RAI

Acknowledgments

SPONSORS:

The President of Ecuador
Metropolitan Touring
Saeta Airlines
Kodak-Comandato S.A.

MAJOR CONTRIBUTORS:

Galápagos Turismo y
Vapores
Quasar Náutica
Tame

Hotel Akros
Hotel Alameda Real
Hotel Colón
Hotel Oro Verde
Hotel Quito
Hotel Sebastián

Banco del Pichincha
Diners Club del Ecuador

Armada Nacional
Ejército Nacional
Fuerza Aérea Ecuatoriana

Alianza Francesa
Conaie
Diario El Comercio
Feprotur
Fundación Natura
Ministry of Foreign Relations

CONTRIBUTORS:

Asociación de Artesanos
Indígenas Salasaca
Cascada de San Rafael
Lodge
Cenecotur
Centro de Rehabilitación de
Mujeres de Imbabura
Centro de Rehabilitación de
Mujeres de Quito
Comunidad Achuar
Comunidad Cofán de
Zábalo
Comunidad Saraguro
Comunidad Secoya de San
Pablo
Comunidad Siona de Puerto
Bolivar
Comunidad Shuar de
Asunción
Convento de la Merced

Convento del Carmen Bajo
Convento del Carmen de la
Asunción
Curia Metropolitana de
Cuenca
Ecuador Amazon Expedition
Ecuavans
Empresa Turística Nacional
Escuela de Arte de la
Universidad Central de
Quito
Escuela Superior Militar
Eloy Alfaro
Flotel Orellana
Galápagos Cruises
Grand Hotel Guayaquil
Hacienda La Avelina
Hacienda San Agustín del
Callo
Hacienda Zuleta
Hostería La Ciénega
Hostería San Francisco
Hotel Atamari
Hotel Casa Blanca
Hotel El Dorado
Hotel El Troje
Hotel La Piedra
Hotel Mirador
Hotel Puerto Lago
M.N. Ambasador
M.N. Santa Cruz
Más y Más
Maternidad Isidro Ayora
Parque Nacional Galápagos
Programa Chicos de la
Calle
Q-Magazine
Refinería Estatal de
Esmeraldas
Revista Vistazo
Safari Ecuador
Taller de Escultura "Las
Cuadras" del IMQ
Taller de Restauración del
Banco Central
Tropical Ecological
Adventures
Universidad Católica de
Guayaquil
Velero Nortada
Yate Encantada

***This project was made
possible through the
extraordinary efforts of
the following people:***

Patrick Barrera
Arturo Crespo Rico
Alicia Durán-Ballén
Eduardo Enmanuel
Andrés Gamio
Eduardo Proaño P.
Jaime Roa
Francisco Valdivieso

SPECIAL THANKS TO:

Juan Aguirre
Rita Aguirre
Diana Andersen
Jorge Juan Anhalzer
Lucia Arízaga
Victor Manuel Bayas
Philippe Ben-Lahcen
Vivian Bibliowicz
Christiane Breustedt
Arturo Cadena
Tania Camacho
Galo Chico
Lucía Chiriboga
Marco Chiriboga
Nicole Coronel
Alberto Croce
Susana Cueva
Max Dahinden
Gustavo De La Torre
Olivier De Quiquerán
Peter Degen
Dolores Diez
Eduardo Diez
Andrew Drumm
Carlina Endara
Armando Espinel
Julio Espinosa
Alejandro Figari
Margarita Gallegos
Marcela García
Enrique Gilardi
Pancho Gilardi
Darío González
Francisco Guzmán
Chuck Halloran
Luis Hidalgo
Alfredo Jarrín
Ann Campana Judge
William Kuykendall
Alberto Luna Tobar

Jamil Mahuad
Zandra Mantilla de Croce
Mónica Martinez
Dean Mills
Silvia Moncayo
Patricio Montaleza
Franz Moser
Karen Myers
Renaud Neubauer
Omar Ospina
Nina Pacari
Patricia Palacios
Rafael Pandam
Cecilia Pérez Huerta
Gustavo Pinto
Toa Quirola
Antonio Ricaurte
Lee Riviera
Juan Carlos Romero
Ricardo Rueda
Francisco Salazar
Zoe Smith
Markus Tellkamp
Roberto Troya
Mercedes de Uriarte
Ernesto Vásquez
Federico Veintimilla
Hernando Velásquez
Nila Velásquez
Oswaldo Viteri
Winston Wlodawsky
George Zacharías
Pablo Zaldumbide

ASSISTANTS TO THE
PHOTOGRAPHERS
AND EDITORS:

Claudia Acosta
Francisco Andrade
Jorge Juan Anhalzer
Marcelo Bahamonde
Vivian Bibliowicz
Camila Bonifaz
Juan Martinez Borrero
Jaime Camacho
Ximena Carcelén
Ann Carey
Mauricio Castillo
Alfredo Chávez
Belisario Chiriboga
Mauricio Cobo
Verónica Cordero
Cristina Cordero
Patrick Costa
Stella De la Torre
Peter Degen

Rodrigo Donoso
Andrew Drumm
Juan Ramón Echevarría
Mariana Garzón
Tanya Klein de Palacios
Pablo Lee
Fausto López
Pablo Lozano
Gonzalo Luzuriaga
Rafael Mashinguiashi
Rohanna Mertens
Lynn Miller
Patricio Montaleza
María José Ospina
Claudia Peralta
Darío Proaño
Paulina Racines
Carla Rossignoli
Armando Salazar
Francisco Salazar
Francisco Torres
María del Carmen
Valdivieso
Andrés Vallejo
Paola Vallejo
Blanca Vega
Cristina Vela
Carlos Villalba
Santiago Viteri

**FRIENDS OF THE
PROJECT:**

Sixto Aguirre
Gabriela Albuja
Laercio Almeida
María Julia de Altamirano
Xavier Alvarado Roca
María Juana Andrango
Rosa María Andrango
Margara Anhalzer
Daniela Arias
Valeria Arroyo
Juan Carlos Avila
Patricia Barrantes
Raul Barreiro
Francisco Beckmann
Michael Bliemsrieder
Cecilia Cabascango
Patricia Cajas
Rosa Elena Camuendo
Alex Canelos
Ana de Canelos
Rómulo Cardenas
María Alexandra Carrillo
Hernán Castro

Tony Castro
Carlos Charri
Lucía Chiriboga
Luz Elena Coloma
Oswaldo Coral
María Eulalia Corral
Norma Corral
Victoriano Criollo
Juan Martín Cueva
Raúl Cushcahua
Germán Dávalos
Terri Davidson
Luz María De La Torre
María de los Angeles
Delgado
Adriana Díaz
Norma Duarte
Carmen Dueñas de
Anhalzer
Freddy Ehlers
Ernesto Estrada
Patricia Estupiñán de
Burbano
Dominique Fall
Eduardo Fernández
Yvette Ferret
George Fletcher
Pedro Freile
Oderay Game
Fernando Garcés
Pablo García
David Gayton
Susana González de Vega
Gustavo González-Lewis
María Eugenia Hidalgo
Carmén Intriago
Arturo Izurieta
Mario Jaramillo
Darwín Jarrín
Arturo Jimenez
Patricia Jurado
Eduardo Kingman
Marcos León
Carmen Luna de Currat
Gino Luzzi
Luis Macas
Patricio Mantilla
José Masaquiza
Jorge Massucco
Fausto Mejía
Juan Molina
Segundo Moreno
Edgar Naranjo
Fernando Navarro
Mónica de Navarro
Alexandra Neira
Jorge Nieto

Patricio Oña
Edwin Orska
Jorge Ortiz
Luís Padilla
Pauline Paimann
Luz del Alba Palacios
Santiago Palacios
Alfredo Pastor
Miñon Plaza
Margarita Plaza de Ponce
Alvaro Ponce
Gonzalo Ponce
María Gloria Ponce
Pedro Proaño
María Eugenia Puente
Querubina Quincheguango
Carlos Quishpe Novoa
Mayer Ramirez
Bernardo Rampón
Lucía Rivas
Byron Rodriguez
Tania Rodriguez
Marcelo Romero
Mario Ron
Eric Rose
Carla Sala
Susana Salgado
Alejandro Santillán
Catalina Sosa
Nicolás Svistoonoff
Mónica Tinoco
Cesar Ubillus
José Vacas
Santiago Valdez
Andrés Valdivieso
Ximena Vallejo
Guiomar Vega
Edmundo Villalba
Rosana Zambrano de Troya